Springtime in Virginia

THE GARDEN   *Morven, Virginia*

Springtime in
VIRGINIA

Photographs by
SAMUEL CHAMBERLAIN

With an Introduction by
VIRGINIUS DABNEY

HASTINGS HOUSE

Publishers   *New York*

12526

INTRODUCTION

VIRGINIA is a land of honeysuckle and beaten biscuit, of bobcats and Lynnhaven oysters, of Smithfield ham and mockingbirds, of roe herring and turkey buzzards. It has some of the richest history and loveliest scenery in the United States.

More and more people are visiting Virginia to see what the State which harbors the site of the first permanent English settlement in the New World is like (Plymouth, Mass., papers please copy). The Old Dominion was jeered at as "fossilized," "moss-backed," and "defunct" as recently as twenty-five years ago, but it has made great strides in the intervening period. Along about 1925 it was said that Virginia had been bequeathed the great landlocked harbor of Hampton Roads by God, and it was apparently waiting for God to develop it. Not so today. Hampton Roads has made long forward strides, and so has the State as a whole.

True, Mr. Arnold Toynbee delivers himself of a pronouncement in his *A Study of History*, which has wrung the withers of Virginians. He cites Virginia, along with South Carolina, as a good example of the "breakdown of a civilization." In contrast, he mentions North Carolina as a virile and up-and-coming state. Now South Carolina can look out for itself, and North Carolina can hardly be blamed for taking a few bows, in view of Mr. Toynbee's eminence, but surely Virginia isn't going to let this sort of nonsense go unchallenged. Mr. Toynbee's memorable howler, in which he speaks of Woodrow Wilson as a North Carolinian, is readily disproved, but his generalizations about the sad state of Virginia civilization are, unfortunately, more difficult to cope with.

When he declares that Virginia "makes the impression of a country under a spell, in which time has stood still," he delivers himself of a declaration which some of the State's more conservative citizens wish were true, but which they know to be inaccurate. To be sure, there are portions of the State, especially in its rural regions, where one can close one's eyes and imagine that he is back in the ante bellum, or even the revolutionary or pre-revolutionary era. But Virginia, as a whole, is not "standing still"; neither can it, despite its faults and shortcomings, be cited as a classic example of a civilization's breakdown. Mr. Toynbee is a scholar of international distinction, but this is one subject on which we believe we are better informed than he. The range of his erudition is amazing, but it evidently does not embrace the cultural, literary, artistic, and economic progress of present-day Virginia. That statement can be made advisedly, and without cheap boosterism or yawping go-getterism.

It must be confessed that we Virginians often take our politics straight, like our whiskey, a condition which contributes to political decay among us. We are further from having a two-party system here than are any of the four states which border on our frontiers, and that is a serious situation. In some sections of the Commonwealth a Republican is almost as hard to find as pterodactyl. Furthermore, there are still tens of thousands of Virginians who apparently would rather vote for Beelzebub than for anybody bearing the label of the GOP, even when the person in question has views much more to their liking than the opposing Democratic nominee. In their hidebound allegiance to a single party they appear to resemble the good burghers of certain far Northeastern states which have been immortalized by the Hon. James Aloysius Farley in his prescient dictum: "As Maine goes, so goes Vermont."

The one-party system in Virginia threatens to rob the Old Dominion of the distinction it has long held, that of being the "Mother of Presidents." Eight occupants of the White House have seen the light in Virginia, as against seven in Ohio. But so long as we remain "in the bag" for the Democrats, no matter who or what is nominated by them, we may as well abandon hope of increasing the number of Virginia-born Presidents to nine. Meanwhile, the title of "Mother of Presidents" is likely to pass to the state of Garfield and Hayes, McKinley and Harding.

Ohio has another claim to fame. At Westerville was the headquarters of the Anti-Saloon League of America, in the days when Bishop James Cannon, Jr., and his pals put Congress through its paces, and anything more potent than one-half of one per cent was considered frightfully intoxicating. During that halcyon era, Virginians were kept well-supplied with "cawn," and the bucolic burble of stills along our creeks was a lullaby for thirsty citizens. Today, Bourbon and branch water or Bourbon and soda is the preferred dish for most of us, unless we belong to the WCTU. Scotia's delectable distillate is less sought after among us than Bourbon. Nor do we go in for rye to any substantial degree, although just across the border in Maryland they inhaust that beverage in much larger quantities than any other type of usquebaugh. However, in the City of Baltimore the populace stows away even vaster quantities of beer than of rye. Herr Mencken's influence doubtless is potent in stimulating the patronage of the Baltimore breweries, for the fabled "Gentleman with the Meat-Ax" has always been a confirmed and consecrated beer-hoister. Yet in Richmond, not many leagues to the South, the preference for Bourbon is of long standing. It is perhaps linked to the sacred julep, which is best made from Bourbon, and is Virginia's gift to the world, all claims to the contrary from Kentucky nevertheless and notwithstanding.

But Virginia has given more than juleps to America. Certainly this Commonwealth has not been as important in more than a century as it was in the late 1700's and early 1800's, but neither was any other American state that important during the same period, nor has any been so important at a later period. It was inevitable that Virginia's position should decline sharply after 1825, but it has not reached the abysmal depths today which its detractors would have you believe. On the contrary, it is one of the most enlightened of the Southern states—in some respects the most enlightened.

For example, Virginia has by far the lowest lynching total since 1882 of any Southern state, with the single exception of North Carolina. These two have had exactly the same number of lynchings during that period—ninety-nine each. Virginia's race relations in other respects are immeasurably better than in many Southern states. The Old Dominion has exhibited considerably greater industrial progress in recent years than most of its sisters which made up the Confederacy, and it has a larger per capita income than almost any. It is better balanced in both industry and agriculture, since in neither category is it largely dependent upon one or two huge industries or crops. The lack of one-crop farming has a direct bearing, too, on the fact that tenancy and share-cropping are considerably less prevalent in Virginia than almost anywhere else in the South. Virginia also is refreshingly free from the Bilbo-Talmadge type of rabble-rouser; indeed, it has never been afflicted with even one such political excrescence. As for the University of Virginia, it is not only the home of the *Virginia Quarterly Review*, one of the finest magazines of its kind, but the University tied with Yale for eighth place in the entire nation, on the basis of a compilation made by the University of Chicago, showing the percentage of university faculties starred in *American Men of Science*. The University of Virginia was ahead of all other Southern institutions in this tabulation, based on the nationally-recognized eminence of scientific faculties, and only .6 behind Harvard.

There are Virginians who boast unduly of their State's great past, and of their own ancestors. Some of these boasts are apocryphal. For example, few Virginians, indeed, are actually descended from the Cavaliers, although there is a widely believed legend to the contrary—a legend carefully nurtured in certain quarters.

Yet many things of which Virginians boast are authentic, and a goodly number of those things may be seen in the splendid photographs which appear in this book: stately "Mount Vernon," graceful "Monticello," white-columned "Arlington"— the mansions of Virginia's great. But we also see in these pages rail fences winding in front of simple farmhouses; the heavens knitting their brows darkly above the Valley of the Shenandoah; the University of Virginia's classic colonnades, silhouetted against the greenery of Spring, and Washington and Lee's grand panorama; the Skyline Drive framed in apple blossoms, and an ancient barn garlanded in dogwood; the miracle of restored Williamsburg, and John Smith, in bronze, looking out upon the rippling James; an old covered bridge near Lexington, of the sort now almost extinct in the State, and fishing nets along the Atlantic shore.

These and countless other scenes go to make up the ensemble that is Virginia. It is an ensemble which in variety and picturesqueness is almost unique. We like to think, too, that the people of Virginia have some qualities that are not always found in profusion elsewhere—courage and pride, integrity and generosity, openhanded hospitality and a tolerance for differing viewpoints. Certainly the early Virginians exhibited these characteristics in marked degree, and among their descendants these qualities are not unknown.

As the State's capital and largest city, and the capital of the Confederacy as well, Richmond naturally enjoys great prestige. Yet in 1786, it was somewhat less impressive. A British traveler named Hunter wrote in his diary in that year a distinctly unflattering description of the town on the hills above the James, and threw in a dig concerning our unpaid debt to the British which sounds, in reverse order, very much like some of the things one hears in this country today. Said Diarist Hunter more than a century and a half ago:

"I rose this morning at eight and after breakfast took a walk about the famous capital of Virginia, which is one of the dirtiest holes of a place I ever was in. . . . Trade is very dull here. The merchants can hardly make it out. . . . The streets are up to your knees in mud almost every step you take in a bad day, and in the summertime you are blinded with dust. . . . The Governor's house is a poor one and the courthouse the shabbiest I ever saw. There are some very pleasant situations upon the hill. Here the Capitol is building. They advance very slowly. I wish instead of laying out their money so ridiculously that they would first pay the British debts, especially when they have so good a statehouse built to their hands in Williamsburg. . . ."

The City of Richmond can afford to laugh today at such outmoded observations. But Richmond is far from being the only notably historic town in Virginia. Fredericksburg and Charlottesville, Lexington and Petersburg, Alexandria and Williamsburg are among the larger places which are known afar, while Jamestown, Yorktown, and Appomattox are smaller, but no less renowned. And there is the sound of bugles in such names as Chancellorsville and The Wilderness, Cold Harbor and Malvern Hill, Cross Keys and Port Republic, Spotslyvania and Yellow Tavern.

Samuel Chamberlain's high sense of art and his virtuosity with the camera have been happily combined in presenting many of the foregoing Virginia scenes, as well as others equally storied, equally charming, in the present volume of photographs. Mr. Chamberlain is a man with an international reputation in the field of photography, and those who view these pictures which he has taken of Virginia will feel that his fame is fully justified. He does not pretend to have covered the whole State, but certainly he has given us some of its grandest vistas and panoramas, some of its most engaging landscapes and perspectives. Virginians will thank him for his rich contribution, and for the integrity and grace with which he has made it.

VIRGINIUS DABNEY

MOUNT VERNON (1743)   *Fairfax County*

SPRING FOLIAGE

Bremo

SHADOWS ON THE OLD FRONT PORCH   *Near Roanoke*

DOORWAY OF KENMORE (1752)   *Fredericksburg*

BERKELEY (1726)   *James City County*

VIRGINIA MANSION   *Richmond*

WAKEFIELD
The Birthplace of George Washington

Westmoreland County

THE OLD LIGHTHOUSE (1791) *Cape Henry*

SPRING BLOSSOMS *Sweetbriar*

THE GARDENS *Brandon*

"GREENWAY"
Birthplace of President Tyler

Charles City County

MICHIE TAVERN (c. 1750)   *Near Charlottesville*

THE MONARCHS

Stratford

THE MEMORIAL AMPHITHEATRE   *Arlington*

THE ROTUNDA   *Charlottesville*

THE WREN BUILDING (1695)
Sir Christopher Wren, Architect

Williamsburg

ST. PAUL'S CHURCH (1739)   *Norfolk*

FRUIT BLOSSOMS   *Skyline Drive*

PORTICO OF THE LIBRARY, UNIVERSITY OF VIRGINIA   *Charlottesville*
Thomas Jefferson, Architect

MONTICELLO (1772)
Thomas Jefferson, Architect

Near Charlottesville

SHIRLEY (1740)   *Charles City County*

WASHINGTON AND LEE UNIVERSITY *Lexington*

FORGOTTEN COLUMNS *Barboursville*

"THE SIGN OF THE GOLDEN BALL"　　　　　*Williamsburg*

WASHINGTON'S MILL   *Near Mount Vern*

THE OLD CEMETERY   *Fredericksburg*

ST. JOHNS CHURCH (1741)
Where Patrick Henry cried "Give me liberty or give me death!"

Richmond

DOGWOOD SILHOUETTE   *Arlington*

COUNTRY ROAD   *Yorktown*

THE GARDEN GATE   *Morven*

PATHWAY TO THE MICHIE TAVERN   *Near Charlottesville*

A COTTAGE AT WAKEFIELD   *Westmoreland County*

THE GARDENS OF MOUNT VERNON

MINOR BUILDINGS AT BREMO

THE OLD PRISON   *Gloucester*

GUNSTON HALL (1758)   *Fairfax County*

THE GARDENS OF GUNSTON HALL   *Fairfax County*

HILLSIDE FARM

Near Natural Bridge

EARLY SPRING AT WESTOVER (1735) *Charles City County*

FARM LANDSCAPE *Near Warrenton*

Portico of the Library, University of Virginia
Thomas Jefferson, Architect

Charlottesville

DUKE OF GLOUCESTER STREET

Williamsburg

CASTLE HILL (1765)   *Near Charlottesville*

IVY-COVERED COTTAGE   *Morven*

RAIL FENCE   *Near Ruckersville*

PICKET FENCE   *Near White Marsh*

THE BUSY SHORE

Hampton

BACK FENCE GOSSIP   *Williamsburg*

COLONNADE — UNIVERSITY OF VIRGINIA *Charlottesville*

MONTICELLO (1772) *Near Charlottesville*

THE PAVILLION

Bremo

MARY WASHINGTON'S HOUSE   *Fredericksburg*

PORTICO OF ARLINGTON (1802)   *Arlington National Cemetery*

THE GREEN — UNIVERSITY OF VIRGINIA   *Charlottesville*

MOUNT VERNON (1743)   *Fairfax County*

FALLS CHURCH (1767)   *Falls Church*

DOGWOOD AT WASHINGTON AND LEE *Lexington*

PORTICO OF THE GOVERNOR'S MANSION   *Richmond*

ORCHARD IN THE RAIN *Near Harrisonburg*

HILLSIDE BLOSSOMS *Near Harrisonburg*

MOUNT VERNON (1743)   *Fairfax County*

MOUNT VERNON FARM BUILDINGS   *Fairfax County*

NATURAL BRIDGE

HICKORY NECK CHURCH   *James City County*

ABINGDON CHURCH (1755)   *Gloucester County*

ASH LAWN
Home of James Monroe

Albemarle County

SHENANDOAH VALLEY FARM

VIRGINIA BEACH

PORTICO OF THE LIBRARY—UNIVERSITY OF VIRGINIA   *Charlottesville*
Thomas Jefferson, Architect

THE WELL   *Williamsburg*

DOORWAY OF THE CARTER-SAUNDERS HOUSE   *Williamsburg*

PORTICO OF THE CAPITOL (1785)
Thomas Jefferson, Architect

Richmond

MOUNT VERNON (1743)   *Fairfax County*

FISHING FLEET   *Hampton*

SPRINGTIME REFLECTIONS   *Diascund Bridge*

WESTOVER (1735) *Charles City County*

THE GARDEN—BRANDON

ARLINGTON (1802)   *Home of General Robert E. Lee*

THE COVERED BRIDGE   *Lexington*

DOORWAY   *Middleburg*

RAIL FENCE   *Near Ruckersville*

WHITEWASHED FARM   *Near Saluda*

JAMES MONROE LAW OFFICE (1758)   *Fredericksburg*

THE CAPITOL

Williamsburg

THE OPEN ROAD   *Near Charlottesville*

THE GORGE   *Natural Bridge*

HIGHLIGHTS ON PEWTER

Morven

CHRIST CHURCH (1773)   *Alexandria*

THE COURTHOUSE (1766)   *Gloucester*

WARE CHURCH (c. 1693)   *Gloucester*

JAMESTOWN NATIONAL MONUMENT

Jamestown

THE LIBRARY, UNIVERSITY OF VIRGINIA
Thomas Jefferson, Architect

Charlottesville

HUGH MERCER APOTHECARY SHOP
The oldest drug store in America

Fredericksburg

KENMORE (1752)   *Fredericksburg*

STRATFORD HALL (1729)   *Westmoreland County*

MOORE HOUSE (1725)   *Yorktown*

THE PYLON   *Arlington*

GEORGE WASHINGTON MASONIC NATIONAL MEMORIAL TEMPLE

Alexandria

WASHINGTON'S GRIST MILL

Near Mount Vernon

ACADEMIC PROMENADE — UNIVERSITY OF VIRGINIA *Charlottesville*

FARM LANE   *Near Middleburg*

THE OLD ARCADE   *Hollins College*

STUDY IN WHITEWASH   *Near Fredericksburg*

HOUSE BY THE ROADSIDE   *Near Fredericksburg*

MARMION   *King George County*

DOORWAY   *Alexandria*

DOGWOOD AT AMPTHILL HOUSE (1732)   *Richmond*

CARTER'S GROVE (1690) *James City County*

SHIRLEY (1740) *Charles City County*

TOMB OF THE UNKNOWN SOLDIER   *Arlington National Cemetery*

THE GARDENS OF MOUNT VERNON

ABINGDON CHURCH (1752)   *Gloucester County*

POHICK CHURCH   *Pohick*

WAKEFIELD
The Birthplace of George Washington

Westmoreland County

DOGWOOD AND DAISIES

Near Charlottesville

THE WATER'S EDGE

Hampton

BERKELEY (1726)   *Charles City County*

PORTICO OF THE CAPITOL (1785)
Thomas Jefferson, Architect

Richmond

THE GOVERNOR'S MANSION

Richmond

OLD CAPE HENRY LIGHTHOUSE (1791)

WEATHERED WHITEWASH   *Near Westover*

BRICK FARMHOUSE   *Lynnhaven*

HILLS ALONG THE SKYLINE DRIVE

THE FARM BUILDINGS AT MOUNT VERNON   *Fairfax County*

THE BACK GATE   *Williamsburg*

THE MANSE
Birthplace of Woodrow Wilson

Staunton

THE LIBRARY

Hollins College

THE WEST FACADE — MOUNT VERNON   *Fairfax County*

ABINGDON CHURCH (1755) *Gloucester County*

MOUNT VERNON FRAMED IN FOLIAGE

Fairfax County

Farm Lane   *Williamsburg*

THE BRICK WALK   *Alexandria*

THE MANSE
Birthplace of Woodrow Wilson

Staunton

MOUNT VERNON (1743)   *Fairfax County*

FARMHOUSE IN THE FOOTHILLS *Shelby*

FARM IN THE SHENANDOAH VALLEY *Near Lexington*

THE OLD APOTHECARY'S SHOP   *Alexandria*

WEST HOUSE (1706)   *Yorktown*

WALTER REED BIRTHPLACE   *Near Gloucester*

THE FARM   *Near Gloucester*

THE MOORE HOUSE (1725) *Yorktown*

SHIELD HOUSE (1699) *Yorktown*

JAMES MONROE LAW OFFICE (1758)   *Fredericksburg*

GUNSTON HALL (1758)   *Fairfax County*

GARDEN OF THE WYTHE HOUSE   *Williamsburg*

DUKE OF GLOUCESTER STREET   *Williamsburg*

THE DOCKS   *Yorktown*

MULBERRY TREE   *Yorktown*

MOORE HOUSE (1725)   *Yorktown*

THE LIBRARY, UNIVERSITY OF VIRGINIA
Thomas Jefferson, Architect

Charlottesville

CARTER'S GROVE (1690)   *James City County*

BUSH HALL (1740)   *Charles City County*

BLOSSOMS IN THE HILLS

Skyline Drive

AQUIA CHURCH (1757)   *Stafford County*

MONTICELLO (1772)
The Home of Thomas Jefferson

Charlottesville

THE BRICK PATH   *Mount Vernon*

THE LEVINGSTON HOUSE   *Williamsburg*

FARM ARCHITECTURE   *Middleburg*

ARLY MORNING CONTRASTS   *Lexington*

THE SENTINEL — WAKEFIELD

Westmoreland County

THE NATURAL BRIDGE

ST. PAUL'S CHURCH

Richmond

ABINGDON CHURCH (1755)   *Gloucester County*

GARDEN GATE   *Stratford*

SERPENTINE WALL — UNIVERSITY OF VIRGINIA   *Charlottesville*

MORNING SHADOWS—MOUNT VERNON (1743) *Fairfax County*

STORM BREWING

Near Staunton

THE GARDENS — STRATFORD

THE STATUE OF JAMES MONROE   *Ash Lawn*

GUNSTON HALL (1758)   *Fairfax County*

TULIPS AND BOXWOOD—GUNSTON HALL

MOUNT VERNON (1743)   *Fairfax County*

MOUNT VERNON   *Fairfax County*

THE ROTUNDA — UNIVERSITY OF VIRGINIA

Thomas Jefferson, Architect

Charlottesville

ST. JOHN'S CHURCH (1728)   *Hampton*

MOORE HOUSE (1725)   *Yorktown*

BANKS OF THE JAMES RIVER   *Jamestown*

WESTOVER (1735)   *Charles City County*

STRATFORD HALL (1729)   *Westmoreland County*

THE GARDENS   *Stratford*

THE ST. GEORGE TUCKER HOUSE *Williamsburg*

SPRING SHADOWS *Williamsburg*

THE MEMORIAL   *Arlington National Cemetery*

COUNTRY CHURCH

Near Leesburg

THE GOVERNOR'S PALACE · *Williamsburg*

THE BANKS OF THE JAMES RIVER *Shirley*

THE SMOKE HOUSE — GOVERNOR'S PALACE   *Williamsburg*

BRUTON PARISH CHURCH (1710-15)   *Williamsburg*

CARTER'S GROVE (1690)   *James City County*

WAKEFIELD
The birthplace of George Washington

Westmoreland County

THE GARDEN WALK — RALEIGH TAVERN   *Williamsburg*

Near Charlottesville

ABINGDON CHURCH (1755)

MONTPELIER (1741)
Home of James Madison

Orange County

THE PIGEON HOUSE   *Brandon*

THE LITTLE STONE HOUSE   *Stratford*

The Natural Bridge in Springtime

KENMORE (1752)   *Fredericksburg*

SABINE HALL (1730)   *Near Warsaw*

OLD PRESBYTERIAN MEETING HOUSE   *Alexandria*

ASH LAWN
Home of James Monroe

Albemarle County

MOUNT VERNON   *Fairfax County*

THE BOTETOURT STATUE (1773)   *Williamsburg*

RIPPON LODGE (c. 1725)

BERKELEY (1726)   *Charles City County*

THE DUNES   *Cape Henry*

COAST GUARD STATION   *Virginia Beach*

RISING SUN TAVERN (c. 1760) *Fredericksburg*

THE GARDEN *Fredericksburg*

THE WOODPILE—MARMION (c. 1674)   *King George County*

THE FARMHOUSE   *Near Aldie*

THE POTOMAC FROM MOUNT VERNON

MARY WASHINGTON HOUSE
Where George Washington's mother lived from 1775 to 1789

Fredericksburg

BEND IN THE ROAD   *Near Leesburg*

CABIN IN THE HILLS   *Near Leesburg*

THE OLD PRISON   *Gloucester*

THE OLD STONE HOUSE   *Richmond*

MARMION (c. 1674)   *King George County*

SIDE STREET   *Alexandria*

THE BANKS OF THE JAMES RIVER   *Jamestown*

FARM BUILDINGS   *Mount Vernon*

GARDEN DETAIL   *Williamsburg*

COACH HOUSE   *Williamsburg*

CREST OF THE HILL—THE SKYLINE DRIVE

THE COVERED BRIDGE   *Lexington*

THE GOVERNOR'S PALACE *Williamsburg*

THE SIR CHRISTOPHER WREN BUILDING (1695) *Williamsburg*

THE RUINS OF ROSEWELL (1725)   *Gloucester County*

WESTOVER (1735)   *Charles City County*

SHADOWS ON WHITEWASH   *Warsaw*

THE STABLES — CARTER'S GROVE

James City County

KENMORE (1752)   *Fredericksburg*

HILLSIDE FARM

Near Ruckersville

THE CAPITOL

Richmond

Thomas Jefferson, Architect

WASHINGTON AND LEE UNIVERSITY   *Lexington*

COVERED BRIDGE   *Lexington*

BLANDFORD CHURCH (1735) *Petersburg*

BREMO

OLD BUILDINGS

Hollins College

WYTHE HOUSE   *Williamsburg*

DOORWAY IN THE GOVERNOR'S PALACE   *Williamsburg*

THE GARDENS OF KENMORE   *Fredericksburg*

DEPENDENCIES OF THE WYTHE HOUSE *Williamsburg*

THE COURTHOUSE (1800)   *Fairfax*

THE OLD BELL TOWER (1824)   *Richmond*

MONTICELLO (1772)
Thomas Jefferson, Architect

Near Charlottesville

THE JAIL DOOR   *Palmyra*

STATUE OF CAPTAIN JOHN SMITH

Jamestown

STATUE OF CAPTAIN JOHN SMITH   *Jamestown*

SPRINGTIME ON THE SKYLINE DRIVE

THE DUKE OF GLOUCESTER STREET   *Williamsburg*

THE WREN BUILDING *Williamsburg*

KENMORE DOORWAY (1752)   *Fredericksburg*

BLOSSOMS ON THE SKYLINE DRIVE

WAKEFIELD
The Birthplace of George Washington

Westmoreland County

STRATFORD HALL (1729)   *Westmoreland County*

VIRGINIA HOUSE   *Richmond*

MOTTLED SUNLIGHT   *Williamsburg*

Date Due

JUL 1 2	AUG 8 '75		
JUL 2 6	OCT 2 1 '75		
AUG 1 7	JUN 7		
	JUL 20 '99		
AUG 2 6			
SEP 2 2			
No 19 '49			
Ap 29 50			
APR 24			
My 9 50			
Ag 25 50			
My 2 51			
Se 13 51			
Ap 24 52			
My 4 56			
No 20 56			
No 26 56			
Oc 31 '57			
SEP 27 '78			
MAY 1 7 '78			